J. L DWELLEY

The Blended Family Guide

Contents

1

Step 1: Marriage

Let no one split apart what God has joined together Mark 10:9. This is one of the staples my wife and I stand on. Being that we had unsuccessful relationships in our past we wanted to put God in the center of everything to assure us that we would never split no matter what we come up against.

One of our top priorities was allowing our children to see love and witness affection between me and my wife day in and day out. It plays a big factor in them buying into whatever ground rules you have in play because they may not be pre-vie to it in their second household.

Communication is a vital step in any relationship but in marriage it's truly your life line. Talk about each other's parenting styles, it may not describe or fix every little thing but you can figure out how each other operates as a parent and be less surprised by their choices later. For instance, in our household I'm the more lenient parent and my wife is more of the disciplinarian, because she's more likely to do the day to day scheduling with the children. There have been times where my wife will try to bring a certain amount of order to how the children's weekday schedule would go as far as dinner and bedtime routine. The children weren't always receptive to how she was trying to bring order in the house which worked best for us. So, we had numerous conversations on how important it was for me and her to be on one accord when it came to the night time routines and as frequently as we stayed on task the children fell right into place.

We definitely felt we were doing the right thing for ourselves and our children, of course there is no way to predict the future but our belief and faith in God trumps anything the devil tries to throw our way. With counsel, family and loved ones around us, we do our best with the information available to us at any given time which is why we try to share our experiences.

Of course like all things, change may be the scariest and there will always be adjustment periods but with Christ in the center of it all you can get through any stage in your blending journey. If you feel the marriage or relationship is right for you, you will soon feel a sense of ease and fall right into alignment with your parenting and co-parenting goals.

My wife and I moved into her mothers house after I sold the house I was currently in and even though we were a family of 6 at that time, you can only imagine what the space was like being in a 3 bed 2 bathroom home. There was quite a bit to get used to but we were determined to make things work. Knowing we were in the process of getting our home built made the sacrifice and determination for our marriage that much more exciting and we were up for the challenge.

Of course we kept it a secret from the kids as they had no idea that our family home that we just made a deposit on was being built, a beautiful 5,100 square foot home with 8 bedrooms and 5 bathrooms. Getting that out the way allowed us to really zone in on the task at hand which was getting our foundation in alignment with being married and juggling the 4 kids we had.

I am a testament to say that if you can last the first two years of marriage, all else will be a cake walk as there were many challenges we faced especially from dealing with the parents on the outside. Staying true to your marriage and standing in the test of time will shape and mold how you want your outcome to look.

We put each other first no matter what it looked like. It's somewhat delusional to most people to hear that you are putting your spouse before everyone including family and children but we made sure to display that type of energy to whomever was around us which makes our marriage going on 7 years the best decisions of my life and I know my wife feels the same, at least that's what she expresses to me all the time . All jokes aside, marriage is work and regardless of what is going on around you including the heavy responsibility and task of being a parent of 6, if you can always stay true to one another in keeping each other first I can almost guarantee nothing can break you.

2

Step 2: Staying on the same page

It was very vital for me and my wife to be on the same page when it came to any and everything. Praying together is one of the tools we use to keep ourselves accountable. We stand on the word 2 Corinthians 6:14, "don't team up with those who don't believe." Believing in the common goal of raising our children in a loving Godly home was our main focus.

Of course if you're in a situation where your exes have not come to terms with your break up it can be harder to have everyone involved on the same page, but this is where prayer and supplication will be key. Not rushing into agreements with parents when emotions are high and you're unable to truly assess the situation from both sides it's best to involve your spouse and God in prayer before making commitments with your exes.

Once you and your spouse have come to an understanding then it's best to bring your ideas to the outside parent. Always remember your primary home comes first. When it comes to the

kids, they will definitely try and get their way by ignoring the step parent and trying to focus their needs and wants on to the immediate parent, so being on one accord plays a huge factor in the kids knowing it doesn't matter what agenda they are trying to push on that parent but nothing chances when both parents made a decision on a rule. Arguments over rules and consequences happen naturally and if you experience any, being on the same page and staying consistent is difficult but very necessary.

Loyalty to your own child or children is definitely a real thing and can feel very strong. This can make discipline for a step parent very delicate at times. As long as you remember that love and trust develops over time between the step parent and step children, you will be fine.

Remember this is all new to everyone so mistakes will happen but as long as your heart's pasture is consistently being checked you can't go wrong. Make sure your intentions, rules and plans come from a pure heart.

I can remember countless times on so many different occasions where the children will try and get me to break or give in to whatever they desire at the moment. For any fathers out there, having a daughter sometimes feels unfair because you almost feel like they can do no wrong and if you are anything like me, I try to give my kids, especially daughters, almost any and everything they want. Not a great idea by the way. So anyway, whenever my wife is out the house running errands or out spending money the kids almost always try to corner me to test my fatherhood. It's almost as if they feel like I'm only stern when Mom is around. I can hear my daughter now " dad, can I play with slime or drink a soda " and if my response is something they don't want to hear they will immediately say " well if mom isn't hear you should be able to allow us to do this or that because you both are our parents and mom shouldn't be the only one with say so " Of course all I can do is laugh, while saying " girl, you know the rules and these are rules me and your mother came up with ".

It also goes the same way when dealing with others outside of your child or children. Me and my wife talk about any and everything and make a decision together on how we want things to go. We've had our slip ups in the past where we made decisions and neglected to tell each other and whenever we find out something after the fact it brought a sense of betrayal to the relationship. I remember a time agreeing with my ex about something without talking to my wife first and vice versa and it would cause friction because it's going against what we try to keep grounded within us. It's always good to have gone through it to see the outcome to learn that ok, I'm not doing that again. So that's why I can't stress enough why it is so important to be sure your children and everyone else knows that as a unit, staying on the same page is a huge key to striving during or throughout this process.

3

Step 3: Mindful of Personalities

It is almost a given that all your kids' personalities will be different. we have them all from shy, to sensitive, to outgoing. Creating boundaries for comfort to each child and how to discipline is also important to how blending can be very effective.

The more they realize your ability to adjust to whatever may be going on with them, the quicker the trust becomes built. Sit down with all the children and explain whatever rules you and your wife or significant other have in play. For the children who are old enough, it's not a bad idea to include them in some decisions to make them feel a little responsible.

Some of the children may not be on board with whatever rules that are in motion but they won't be shocked or thrown off by whatever rules that are communicated. We have a son who is my bonus son that is passionate about any and everything he is doing and is very competitive. He doesn't like to lose at anything and when he does, the sensitivity just

7

comes out and man looks out! And you can almost sense his frustrations right away because he just shuts down and gets upset. I say that to say, even disciplining him can be very tricky and me and my wife try to reason with him at all times because if you're too hard on him or yell at him about something, he almost zones you out and in the end we really didn't get through to him because of his attitude.

So disciplining your children differently depending on their personalities is very crucial if you're trying to get them to understand what they did wrong. Our oldest daughter is a bit sensitive as well, a lot more when she was younger but my wife and her have a very open communication which is a beauty to watch. She talks to her about everything which makes it easier for her to come to us about anything she may be feeling or experiencing and if there is anything I can express about that, it's that being open with your child and allowing them to express how they feel allows them not to keep too many secrets from you. We all have been accustomed to doing that with our parents when we were younger.

Now the elementary kids we have are our firecrackers, they have more energy than superman himself. Although it can be taxing with the amount of discipline it takes for them because of their age and so much growing and learning that they have to do, it's just as important which is why they probably get the most reprimand out of all the children.

Our three year old daughter that me and my wife share together is a handful and she tries to use her shyness and fake tears to to get away with God knows what, but her and her younger sister are in the clear because me and my wife can have our way with them and of course they aren't old enough to really understand why their older siblings from time to time aren't at home they are with the other parents on the outside.

Of course we will cross that bridge when the time comes but all in all different personalities just come with it and being mindful of that in all situations won't do anything but help, trust us - we have the experience to back it up.

4

Step 4: Respect& Support

It's almost impossible to not have respect for everyone involved in your blended family. Even though past relationships didn't work out on a personal level when children are created you have to immediately place your emotions into check and respect the other person for who they are, which is a parent to your child.

Respecting the parents authority is key to getting the support that is needed to have a common goal which is the emotional wellbeing of the child that's involved. My wife and I had to do this on 4 different levels. What we understand is everyone's household is different and everyone's mindset when it comes to family is different, so when there are times when we want to put our plans and expectations to the forefront we almost immediately ask ourselves this vital question, " How would what we want to do benefit the child?". Your main focus should and always should be how can we help our child in this limited time we have to make an impression on their lives. What we must always remember is that children grow up! They don't always stay in that young and immature state all of their lives, and if your raising them correctly, which I know you are if your seeking assistance and buying books to educate yourself on this topic, respecting the other parents and working together for the betterment of your child and your complete family is essential and support from all parents will come naturally.

One thing me and my wife hang our hats on is the importance of not bashing the other households' ways because it will and can definitely cause friction which will not result in anything positive and could cause long term stress and unnecessary issues that will only hurt the child .

Even if there could be an issue or a problem that may arise, allowing the child to feel like there aren't any underlying issues with the other side is always best. Whether you have a great relationship with your ex or a terrible one, that person is going to be a part of your family as long as you're involved with the child you two share. Just like your ex will be a part of your family, you're going to need to accept your spouse's ex into the family as well.

As difficult as it may be at times, it's going to be essential to your family's overall health and the relationship with your bonus children. When the children spend the week or weekend with you, try not to be the " fun house " in an attempt to be liked or favored by the child or children.

This can create tension or a problem between you and the other household because they may have a hard time transitioning back. Me and my wife have both faced challenges when dealing with the other side. There have been times where it has gotten extremely difficult and stressful and I decided to go the route of anything that reduces stress and what I found out was that peace was the best outcome in any situation for me and things got better for me once I decided not to argue or fight with my children's mothers regardless of who was in the wrong.

My wife went through similar situations but being the primary parent, she almost always gets the upper hand but our game plan remains the same and we always decide to go the route that causes the least amount of trouble or tension.

For the most part all of the kids' parents on the outside are cordial with us all and we try to put the benefits of the kids at the forefront of any and everything. When it comes to birthday parties, school functions or even their extra curricular activities, we all show up and support them at all costs and I think the kids seeing that just makes things flow a lot more smoothly.

Always be mindful of not engaging conversations with outside people which could result in words going back to the other party. My wife has realized a-lot of people love to want to know what's going on just so they can go back and tell something that wasn't meant the way they expressed it. So we are always mindful of not talking to anyone other than ourselves about our children's parents on the outside.

I remember as a child, I would often think if my parents didn't like or talk to someone or if I even had an inkling that there was an issue that it was evident that I should have a problem with that same person. I say that to say that I seem to feel that way with our children where I don't want them to feel those feeling at all which is why me and my wife not only gets along with the other side but we demonstrate that to the kids in showing them that there is never and issue with the other side and we always speak positivity as well even if it may not always be a positive situation.

There will never be a time where our kids can go outside of our home into their other homes to tell the parent that we were speaking negatively or even remotely being disrespectful and in turn we will always receive that same respect. I'm not at all saying that you have to be friends or invite one another over for Christmas or Thanksgiving dinners but in order for the blending to be successful, there definitely has to be a level of respect between both parties or families and that's what we hang our hats on day in and day out.

5

Step 5: Relationships among the children

Treating all the kids the same is something that should probably be most important in the household and them seeing the opposite will not sit well with them or the parents on the other side.

The best way to keep the relationship positive is to live by the code, "if this was me how would I want to be treated." We live by the word of God and we live by Godly principles and the main one we always tell our children, is you reap what you sow. Wow, think about that in its simplest form. You put in what you get out. If you consistently put in toxic behaviors, words and responses, please understand that you will get that in return.

We have all heard the term " being treated like the stepchild ", which I personally disliked because my wife was a step child and she would tell me her experiences and stories that would make one cry. I had to make sure when put in that position that I changed the narrative of what a "step child" looked like.

You never want to make any child feel less than the other so loving them all the same should not only be a priority but necessary. Try not to push them into being your best friend.

Follow your bonus children's lead in deciding how to interact with them. Having open communication and conversations about their feelings is important to getting to know them better. Our bonus children on each side were so open to getting to know the new parent, it could have had a lot to do with age. My bonus son was 6 years old when I came into his life and my daughter was 8 years old when my wife came into her life. At that young age both children were shy at first with interactions but we kept them in a place of open communication, taking them to parks and sporting events so they can interact with their friends as well as see how we interacted with them individually and together.

The kids could easily get into a space where they feel it's a rivalry or competition against the others, so it's important to step in before it goes too far.

It can be fun in the beginning about acquiring new family members but once the dust settles they could pick fights with one another because of having to share space or attention with the siblings they don't know too well yet. Our advice is to keep them together.

Both me and my wife had siblings growing up and what we noticed is that it is natural for siblings to disagree and fight so know what comes with it. Keep the kids together but get them to understand they must respect each other and when in the house together spacing them out isn't always a bad idea just don't disciple one without the other.

We would always have a term called "group disciple" for instance if one got in trouble they both got in trouble to keep them keeping their simple complaints to themselves allowing them to use some problem solving techniques. In the beginning of our living situation we were in a very small house so we could hear how the children spoke to one another and we made sure their words weren't offensive and disrespectful. We corrected them alot!

All normal behaviors but once they understood the words they can and can't use their language and tone changed and the relationships got better over time.

6

Step 6: Affirmation

In our family we always try to teach the kids that they are indeed brothers and sisters and are family and teaching them how important it is to love one another, so constantly telling them that reassures them.

Of course like most great things it takes time to create and build as you are constantly learning to work together and care for everyone involved.

It's extremely important to know that you won't always have the answers and things will not always go according to whatever plan you may have in place and this is ok, however consistency is key! Being consistent in your words when addressing your children publicly or to family or friends ensures those around you know how you see your bonus child or children.

My wife and I reference all the children the same. We don't have labels like step or bonus to outside people because we see our family as one! As the number of children increase, as it frequently does in blended families, one or most of the children might feel like they aren't getting the attention they once had.

Giving each child individual attention helps as well, whether it is playing a quick game together or just any sort of one on one interaction, giving the kids plenty of positive attention can strengthen your bond with them.

We have our children in all kinds of activities ranging from basketball, football, cheerleading, and softball and I make sure I do a little of everything with each child whether it's getting some shots up with him on the basketball court, throwing the football around, help working on dance routines or even playing a little softball. So that definitely is a plus giving them that extra one - on - one time in assuring they are loved and noticed

7

Step 7: Routines

I t's very imperative that you try and have a good routine in place so that everything can run as smoothly as it can as things can get hectic and stressful.

My daughters primary home was 30 mins away from the home me and my wife built. We were on a week on week off with her, and if we didn't keep our routine things could naturally get overwhelming. We had to be mindful of our time everyday because we had to tack on a 45 minute ride to her school daily on the weeks we had her. It took an adjustment period for everyone in the house. Our children in the house had to wake up earlier and go to bed earlier in those weeks. What got our kids excited and accepting of our routine was that we were truly involved as husband and wife. We had family meetings once in those weeks. She was in the house to get the kids to interact with us about their feelings and ideas.

These family meetings became the catalyst of our core values. We would do children's Bible story readings on those nights and pray as a family nightly and it really set a core fundamental principle in our children. They were able to see both my wife's and I heart for God, each other and then as children in a family. We wanted to install in our children Godly principles for living by his word. My wife and I always talk about our strategies before bringing them to the kids.

Try not to engage too much into being a stern parent - I often myself look at it as if I were an adult baby sitter or a big brother. Staying clear about your role will help the children understand how their new family fits together so always be sure to stay consistent.

When your kids feel like they are getting their emotional needs met and they aren't losing you to the family you guys are trying to build, they might feel better about just buying in and going with the flow. If you're used to going by their favorite park or ice cream shop every Friday after school, keep it up.

My wife loves holidays and does certain things like bake cookies on Christmas Eve every year, continuing that and remembering it will be even more special to them because it's something they will be looking forward to.

8

Step 8: Managing Emotions

T he definition of emotion is a natural instinctive state of mind deriving from one's circumstances, mood, or relationships with others.

Relationships with others is one of the main factors of our emotions, so managing them will be one of the essential guidelines to having a successful blending relationship with all parties involved. This is easier said than done. Emotions are tricky when you think something doesn't bother or frustrate you.

One word or action can throw you completely off and cause you to react or respond in a way you weren't expecting. Unmanaged emotions can have you saying and doing things that will have a long lasting damaging effect on your life.

You've seen it, an upset employee comes to work and hurts themselves or others because they didn't receive the respect they thought they desired on a job, or children going to school and hurting one another because they were bullied about something that was out of their control.

These are unmanaged emotions. That caused a lasting effect on one's life. In this instance we're talking about a family which I don't know which is more permanent in one's life. The family you have will be your family forever until you're no longer living on this earth.

Your family is a staple in who you are as a human being. You want the people closest to you to respect your position in their lives so the only way you can obtain this is by managing your emotions and your actions to follow those emotions.

Being we are all human it is easy to show emotion when things don't necessarily go your way while parenting which is why being intentional and in control of situations is always the safest bet. I was definitely emotional whenever I assumed something rather than talking with my wife about what may have occurred with our children.

Communication is key when figuring out how to manage your emotions. If you don't talk about what is going on in your head then don't expect a change in your circumstances. As long as communication is at the forefront, dealing with the child or children about a situation will be effortless when the parents can tackle it together in getting them to understand.

Be honest with your partner about how you're feeling. There is a good chance they may have some of the same concerns, and if so, it could bring you closer together.

9

Step 9: Co-Parenting

This may be the most important step of them all when dealing with the co parent outside of your home. Always be mindful of how they may feel as long as it doesn't affect your household or change any dynamics you have for your home.

Oftentimes depending on what feelings or reserves the other parent may have, it could seem as if they can be difficult about certain or most things but I can assure you if you stay consistent in whatever lifestyle you display in your blending of the children, things will get in line when you least expect it.

As busy as you may be trying to make blended family work, it's just as important not to forget to also stay dedicated to co - parenting with your ex. Oftentimes it's overlooked but co parenting has a significant impact on your day to day life and can't be ignored.

It's always helpful to have great techniques to make things flow more naturally and smoothly. If plans change and things come up, always be mindful of notifying your ex if it's something that can impact your child in any way

Now you don't have to share private details, but they will likely appreciate knowing when something has changed in your plans that the child was a part of, before hearing about it on social sites, or through mutual friends. I try to be as helpful as I can with making life easier on my children's mothers whether it be financially or physically in helping in any way I can.

Me and my wife literally find ways to help one another when it comes to managing time which is the biggest obstacle we face.

So staying on top of our children's schedule is really what we pride ourselves on because we know staying consistent keeps everything intact. It's really about being a team with the outside parents, everyone's heard the term it takes a village to raise children and that is nothing far from the truth.

Things always come up in your everyday planning so whether it's a custody agreement you may have or not, being present and available for the children should always trump whatever a judge says has to be done. I do have a custody agreement with my daughter's mother but we don't abide by it at all because we do what's best for our daughter at any given time.

Me and my wife literally help our daughters mother with any assistance she may have which makes co-parenting effortless. We put our children's needs above our own all the time and it's what you have to do in order to stay consistent in how you want your blended families to thrive.

When holidays come around, making plans for the children and being in communication with the other side is very vital as well. If we know we don't have much of a plan on doing something, it's never an issue for them to spend time with their other family and vice versa.

Try not to ever make things difficult because in the end it will only affect the child. We always allow our children to voice their opinions on what they would like to do, especially our teenagers. We try not to force anything on them as all it will do is cause frustration and anger with everyone involved. It is just as important to keep your exes in the loop with certain things pertaining to the children you share just to eliminate surprises that might rub them the wrong way.

Although we trust the parents on the other side to always do things in the best interest of the child, that may not always be their mentality they have toward you on your side. So again, as long as you can be mindful to keep an open discussion about plans you may have with your children's parents, the better the outcomes of co-parenting will be.

Step 10: Avoiding Conflict

Displaying favoritism toward your biological children will definitely be something the bonus children will realize almost right away.

You may have a different kind of connection with your own kids but the bonus children should never feel that they are being treated poorly or being ignored.

Me and my wife try not to do anything different with one child over the other and we always try our best to treat them equally so it's always best to stay aware of the messages you're sending to avoid hurt feelings because it can last a long time. Always remember your children may be more like strangers than siblings (usually in the very beginning) so don't expect everyone to be one big happy family. It will always take some time to get to that point.

Me and my wife have been together for 7 years now and married 6 and were at a place where all the kids consider themselves as siblings but it didn't happen overnight.

Avoid placing labels on kids, even positive labels like he is the athlete of the family or she is the fast and bright one because it can increase tension or even jealousy or envy among siblings. Point out that each and everyone one of them have many skills and talents. It is almost always evident whenever there is tension among siblings whether they are playing a game at home, eating dinner or even watching tv.

Whenever I see a problem arise I try to get on top of it immediately and get to what may have caused it to occur. As you all may have witnessed with children, it can go from fun, fun, fun to why are they even here in a matter of seconds which is why me and my wife always try to do things with the kids that may be beneficial to all of them.

We try to have conversations with one another frequently so they can express their trigger points and get them to interact with one another nicely. Even allowing them to get out of the house and do things they enjoy could bring their bonds closer.

We never assume everything is all good and you shouldn't as kids and their emotions fluctuate as the situation changes. Love and consistency will always be the trick to being able to weather storms that may arise when it comes to your children because as soon as they see something different is when you leave the door open for them to feel they can behave poorly.

One of my favorite acts of discipline whenever I can sense some sort of frustration within the child or children was to send them to their rooms so they can be alone while everyone else interacted with one another. Works every time in getting them to understand getting their emotions in line is necessary. Remember you won't always avoid conflict when dealing with children but if you manage your emotions and have intentional interactions all your encounters will be genuine.

www.ingramcontent.com/pod-product-compliance
Lightning Source LLC
Chambersburg PA
CBHW071504150726
48000CB00006B/2689